Janet Cardiff
&
George Bures Miller

The House Of Books Has No Windows

VOLUME I
selected works

PUBLISHED BY
THE FRUITMARKET GALLERY, EDINBURGH
MODERN ART OXFORD

Contents

Foreword

FIONA BRADLEY
THE FRUITMARKET GALLERY
SUZANNE COTTER & ANDREW NAIRNE
MODERN ART OXFORD

Janet Cardiff and George Bures Miller are internationally renowned for their collaborative multimedia installations that engage all the viewer's senses in the creation of parallel worlds. *The House Of Books Has No Windows* is an exhibition made for The Fruitmarket Gallery, Edinburgh and Modern Art Oxford that brings together seven installations made by Cardiff and Miller between 1995 and 2008. The art of storytelling, inspired as much by *film noir* as by the short stories of Jorge Luis Borges and Franz Kafka, underpins much of the artists' work, and this present project, in a number of ways.

Cardiff credits literature rather than visual art as a key inspiration, and all of the installations in the exhibition – from the narrative mechanisms at play in the collection of objects and ephemera in *The Dark Pool*, to *Opera for a Small Room*, an installation of 2,000 records, 8 robotically controlled record players and 24 speakers, and the *The Killing Machine*, inspired by Kafka's chilling short story *In the Penal Colony* – attest to this. The newest work in the exhibition, *The House Of Books Has No Windows*, is a house made entirely of books. Spines out, pages in, the work is a library turned in on itself, a space of infinite possibility where nothing may be read yet everything imagined.

Fiction permeates the project deeper than this, however. Early in its genesis, Cardiff and Miller proposed that the publication accompanying the exhibition should take the form of a compendium of unrealised – as yet fictional – works, and the second volume of this publication is the realisation of this. Selected from notebooks kept by Cardiff and Miller individually over the last 18 years and published as they come, a notebook page to a page, the projects offer a range of routes in to the Cardiff/Miller imagination. Some are the briefest of sketches, others more worked-up ideas. Some are clearly early thoughts for works that were later realised, while others, still technically unrealisable, may well remain forever in the realm of fiction.

The work *The House Of Books Has No Windows*, as well as lending its title to the exhibition, links the second volume of the publication, the compendium of unrealised works, to this one, the catalogue of works in the exhibition. The piece has its genesis in the selection of unrealised projects – it first surfaced in a 1996 notebook of Cardiff's. Its realisation for the exhibition came out of discussions around the fictional projects for inclusion in the publication.

At The Fruitmarket Gallery and Modern Art Oxford we are pleased and proud to have worked with Janet Cardiff and George Bures Miller on the preparation of this exhibition. We are grateful to Richard Calvocoressi and The Henry Moore Foundation, the International Cultural Relations Division at Foreign Affairs and International Trade Canada (DFAIT) and The Canada House Arts Trust for their much-appreciated financial assistance; to the artists' galleries Luhring Augustine in New York and Barbara Weiss in Berlin for their practical support during the making of the exhibition; and to Kitty Scott, Director of Visual Arts at The Banff Centre, for her help and advice. Outset Contemporary Art Fund supported the production of the exhibition's eponymous work *The House Of Books Has No Windows*. We are grateful to them for their enlightened approach to contemporary art patronage.

Thanks are also due to Jules Youngberg, the artists' young nephew, whose short story ends this volume of the publication. A journey into the work from a particularly personal perspective, his is another story through which to approach the art of Janet Cardiff and George Bures Miller. Theirs is a singular project, and one which we believe will speak with a resonant voice to our audiences. Above all, we offer Janet and George our heartfelt thanks – for their collaboration and commitment to this exhibition, and for their wonderful work, which inspires and transports us in ways we could not have imagined.

The House of Books Has No Windows

✠

Storytelling:
Recent collaborative installations by
Janet Cardiff and George Bures Miller

FIONA BRADLEY

✠

Tell me muse, storyteller, he who has been thrust to the edge of the world both an infant and an ancient, and through him reveal Everyman. With time, those who listened to me became my readers. They no longer sit in a circle, but apart, and one doesn't know anything about the other. I'm an old man with a broken voice but the story still rises from the depths and the slowly opened mouth repeats it as clearly as it does powerfully, a liturgy for which no one needs to be initiated to the meaning of the words and sentences.[1]

WINGS OF DESIRE, 1987

Wim Wenders' ageing author thinks these thoughts in the Berlin public library. Wenders' film *Wings of Desire*, with its gentle, eavesdropping angels, its layering of history and memory, fact and fiction, and its insistence on the power of story, is a favourite of Janet Cardiff's and George Bures Miller's, and the library as a place where people and ideas meet is a powerful image for them – 'I love libraries because of the layers of time and meaning they contain. I like how you can escape into other worlds in a library, how when you open a book, you're somewhere else'.[2] Escaping into other worlds is one of the principal operations of their work – in 2004, Cardiff wrote 'I've always loved to escape, whether it was through walks, books, films or dreams, and it's only now that I realise what I've been doing this past decade. I've been creating portholes into my other worlds'.[3]

Cardiff wrote this in the context of her walks, the works with which she first came to prominence in the early 1990s. Taking the form first of a Walkman, then a CD Walkman, and now an iPod, the walks invite the viewer to don a headset, press play and follow in Cardiff's footsteps, retracing a journey that she made some time before, and entering a strange new time and place as the sights and sounds of the real world merge with the recordings and imaginings of the piece. Alongside the walks, however, Cardiff has also always made installations, and it is these, specifically those made in collaboration with George Bures Miller, that concern us here. Much of the power of the walks is shared by the installations, in particular the immediacy of communication, the sense that the artists might be, in Wenders' words, 'thinking as if [they were] talking to someone else', or indeed that we are listening as though eavesdropping on their thoughts.

Cardiff and Miller's collaborative installations are multi-layered, multimedia experiences. Using objects, images and, crucially, sound, they collage together impressions and experiences, memory and history, mixing references to high and popular culture in works that exist in a time and rhythm all their own. They are time-based – that is, they run for a particular length of time – but they are open-ended and ambiguous, leaving space for the viewer to occupy them and interact with them, both imaginatively and practically.

Road Trip (2004), an installation that takes the form of an automated slide talk, seems to enact the processes by which Cardiff and Miller make their work, and we as viewers experience it. It runs continuously, a carousel of slides clicking through, accompanied by a loop of audio in which Cardiff and Miller discuss first the slides, then the possibility of making a work with the slides – the work we are watching:

G: Why did you have that one out of order?

J: I don't know.

G: Because now we're back in the mountains. It doesn't make sense. It should go from the mountains to Calgary to the prairies…

J: This is sort of prairie.

G: This looks like Northern Ontario to me, that sort of swampy wasteland.

J: This is definitely prairie though…

G: This is badly organised.

J: Well…

G: I mean I thought this was about a road trip. We're supposed to be trying to get across this idea of crossing the country and you're skipping all over the place. Like the two shots of the lake… that's Lake Superior again, that should be with the other shot of Lake Superior.

J: Well, somehow they got out of order, OK?

G: I mean, we're supposed to be developing a storyline here, and there's no storyline…

J: Well, do you want to re-order them right now?

G: I guess so. It's a lot of work…

In the course of the piece it becomes clear that the slides are from a collection taken by Miller's grandfather during a trip from Calgary to New York City. Miller's grandfather died before he was born, and Miller and Cardiff's collaborative squabbling is interspersed with speculation as to why some film stock has aged better than others; how it is that photographs taken by someone can tell you something about them; and what kind of man he was ('I wonder if that's him?'). The piece dips in and out of reality – you hear Cardiff and Miller walking around the space, being distracted by extraneous sounds, re-ordering the slides. In the end, though, it's all about levels of reality – though the voices we hear are recognisably the voices of Cardiff and Miller, we cannot be sure if it is a real conversation we are hearing or a script. Early on in her practice Cardiff invented a fictional 'Janet', a woman with her voice and her name who inhabits her work but is not necessarily her, and so it is presumably with George also. Yet we cannot help the feeling that we are hearing a real conversation, and that the work is in some way a sketch for or vignette of the artists' real working relationship, and this is in fact the case. The artists recorded the conversation they had while looking through the slides in preparation for a much larger piece. It was only when they listened back to the recording together with the synchronised slides that they realised it could work as a piece on its own.

Cardiff has said that *The Dark Pool* (1995) is 'the perfect kind of collaboration. It mixes his sense of that strange library aesthetic with technology – kind of cyberpunk but engaged with technology – with my interest in bringing the labyrinth of stories into it. The two aesthetics merge into one big story'.[4] If *Road Trip* purports to provide an insight into Cardiff and Miller's working relationship, then it is easy to imagine that *The Dark Pool*, with its books, record players, speakers, models, notes, drawings and peculiar mechanical devices, owes something to the reality of their studio. The work takes the form of a room full of stuff, seemingly abandoned. Opening an old door, we feel we are trespassing on the workspace of some kind of mad scientist or investigative writer. As we move round, we trigger sounds – stories, conversations, music – that speak of the 'dark pool', a mysterious place where people disappear. As in *Road Trip*, there is a moment when the characters of Janet and George speak directly to each other, and seemingly to us:

J: Just tell me what you see.
G: There's nothing there, just a few shadows.
J: But…there was something there yesterday.
G: Like what?
J: He said that he could see the shadows of two people dancing.
G: I don't see anything.
J: They're in front of the tables, and they're waltzing round the room. Her head's on his shoulder, and you can tell by the way he holds her that he loves her.
G: That's a nice story. I'm sorry I don't see it.

In making *The Dark Pool* Cardiff and Miller have said that they wanted to 'haunt the space with an invisible presence. We littered the space with traces of inexplicable activities and objects to provide clues as to whom might have lived there and what they had been doing. We hoped to create an environment that removed the viewer from the art gallery and transported them into another space and time so that they forgot where they were and why they had come. Maybe they had slipped through the back door into an abandoned warehouse, into a world where their slightest movement could stir up the dusty memories into sounds and stories that they could hear as they moved through the space'.[5] The work taps into that sense we have that historically, or otherwise, resonant spaces have their past somehow close to the surface, that if we only knew how to tap into them we could hear conversations and see events that happened there long ago. Not exactly theatrical, like many of Cardiff and Miller's works, this piece speaks more of an abandoned film set, a place where action either may have happened or may be about to happen, where we can eavesdrop on the future or the past.

The *Muriel Lake Incident* (1999) is theatrical, and is something of a precursor to *The Paradise Institute*, the fully-operational mini movie theatre Cardiff and Miller presented in the Canadian Pavilion at the Venice Biennale in 2001, which brought their collaborative installation work to international attention. *The Muriel Lake Incident* is a large plywood box, into which the viewer is invited to peer. The box is a cinema, seen in hyper-perspective, with seats and a tiny screen showing a five-minute, Midwestern *film noir*. We wear headphones and watch the film. Many of film's classic tropes are there: a car driving, a dark-haired woman dancing, a hallway with doors to open, references to Orson Welles, a threatening stranger, suspenseful music, gunshots. Several of them, however, happen not in the filmed action, but in the cinema – phantom fellow audience members speaking directly into our ear: 'This isn't the film I thought. Wasn't it supposed to be directed by Orson Welles?... This is too weird. She looks just like the woman in my dream last night. I was walking down a hallway and I opened a door into a room... Did you see that crazy man outside the theatre? I think he's sitting behind us...' The piece ends in gunshots, but in the cinema, not on the screen – the mix of 'real' and 'filmed' action is complete.

The Muriel Lake Incident is made using a technique of sound recording known as binaural recording. This is the technique behind the uncanny aural accuracy of Cardiff's walks, and involves recording on two microphones at once, situated in the ears of a dummy head. The result, when played through headphones, mimics the way we actually hear sound, and is so authentic that the recorded sound and the actual present sound become confused. When the woman in the audience whispers in our ear while watching *The Muriel Lake Incident*, it is impossible not to turn round to see who is talking to us. Binaural recording creates space and time as well as sound: it gives an eerily accurate sense that we are occupying a space other than the one we actually are (the sound in *The Muriel Lake Incident* was recorded in a full-scale cinema, hence our conviction while we are standing in the gallery watching the piece that we actually are in a cinema); and it enables us to measure time according to that other space – when we hear people walk away from us across a large space, the time they take is the imagined time of the world of the piece, not the real time of the art gallery. This ability to mix and mix up time and space is what draws Cardiff and Miller to sound – Cardiff has commented: 'I'm not interested in media for media's sake. I'm not interested in experimental electronic music or abstract sound art. I'm interested in taking the technology, seeing what it can do, using it and manipulating it for conceptual reasons'.[6] '...The way we approach audio is very similar to printmaking. I was trained as a printmaker and practised up to the nineties. You can take different sources from all over and then collage them together. Conceptually I always found that interesting: you can take something recorded now, and footage that was recorded 20 years ago, and you can seamlessly put them together in audio. It's like a mixture of time and space'.[7]

Opera for a Small Room (2005) begins with the sound of an orchestra warming up and ends with the sound of clapping. Sounding as though it was recorded in a large concert hall, the applause immediately puts the viewer conceptually into a performance space, waiting for the work to start. The piece consists of the small room of the title, first made in and then ripped out of the artists' present studio. The room looks like a cross between a garden shed and a packing crate – it is a roughly-made structure, with a large central window and two side windows into which viewers can look, but no door. Inside the room is a huge collection of records, several record players and a bewildering number of antique speakers. The artists found the records, all opera, and all the property of one R. Dennehy, in a second-hand sale in Salmon Arm in rural British Columbia. Like the slides in *Road Trip* and the artefacts in *The Dark Pool*, the records set the stage for an elaborate investigation into the relationship between the collector and the things collected, into the identity of R. Dennehy as glimpsed through his choice of records.

The investigation is conducted through sound. The room performs a 20-minute opera, building up sound in layers until the entire room is throbbing, lights flashing in time with the rhythms. The sound is a collage of opera, rock music, a recording of a stage hypnotist from the 1970s, the sound of rain and a train, and the lonely musings of the opera-lover in his room: 'This place is falling apart. The animals are taking over. The weasels eat the mice and the squirrels. The mice are chewing on the wires in the walls. If they start on the records I'll have to poison them…' It appears to come from the records and record players in the room, and is incredibly authentic – so much so that as a train goes past it seems inevitable that the chandelier should shake, and the sound of drumming rain makes the space feel cold and vulnerable. The piece transports the viewer to rural Canada so completely ('the sun was on the cliffs as I drove past the feed plant') that the applause at the end pulls us up short, returning us abruptly to reality, albeit the reality not of the gallery, but the aurally-constructed concert hall.

In *Opera for a Small Room*, we eavesdrop, like Wenders' angels, on a man's life, his identity reconstructed through his passion for opera. In *The Killing*

Machine (2007), we are altogether more implicated, invited to start a machine inspired partly by the artists' hatred of the American system of capital punishment, and partly by Franz Kafka's hideous short story *In The Penal Colony* (1919). Like the explorer in the story, we are forced to take an active part in the operation of the machine – like *Opera for a Small Room*, it then performs for us, but its performance, though beautiful, is chilling. And this time the sound it makes does not transport us elsewhere – made in the room, by a guitar hit by a robotic wand, it forces us to stay in the room with it.

If *The Killing Machine* withholds the possibility of escape, *The House Of Books Has No Windows* (2008) is all about it. Little more than an idea at the time of writing (the drawing that inspired it was one of the unrealised projects selected for the companion volume to this book), the piece returns us to Cardiff's image of a library as a repository of other worlds. The piece – a house made out of a collection of books, a domestic library turned inside out – puts the viewer at the sharp end of a book's transportative power. The piece has no windows and no sound – in the absence of external stimulation, we must imagine the worlds of the books, and hear the voice in our head that talks to us when we read. This voice is for me the voice of Cardiff and Miller's work – the voice of memory, of history, of the imagination, the voice of the story that still rises from the depths.

NOTES

1.   *Wings of Desire*, 1987, Wim Wenders (director), Wim Wenders and Peter Handke (writers), Richard Reitinger (screenwriter).

2.   Janet Cardiff in conversation with Carolyn Christov-Bakargiev in Anthony Huberman (ed.), *Janet Cardiff: A Survey of Works including Collaborations with George Bures Miller*, P.S.1 Contemporary Art Center, New York, 2001.

3.   Janet Cardiff, 'The First Page', in *The Walk Book*, Thyssen Bornemisza Art Contemporary, Vienna and Public Art Fund, New York, 2005.

4.   Janet Cardiff in conversation with Carolyn Christov-Bakargiev, op. cit.

5.   Janet Cardiff, untitled statement, in Carolyn Christov-Bakargiev, op. cit.

6.   Janet Cardiff in conversation with Carolyn Christov-Bakargiev, op. cit.

7.   Janet Cardiff in 'Janet Cardiff and George Bures Miller interviewed by Michael Juul Holm', in Michael Juul Holm and Mette Marcus (eds.), *Louisiana Contemporary. Janet Cardiff and George Bures Miller*, Louisiana Museum of Modern Art, Humlebæk, 2006.

The Killing Machine
2007

Mixed media/audio installation
pneumatics/robotics

5 minutes

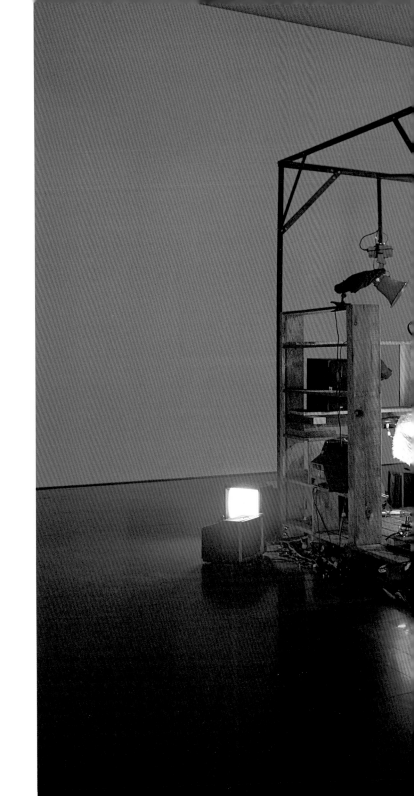

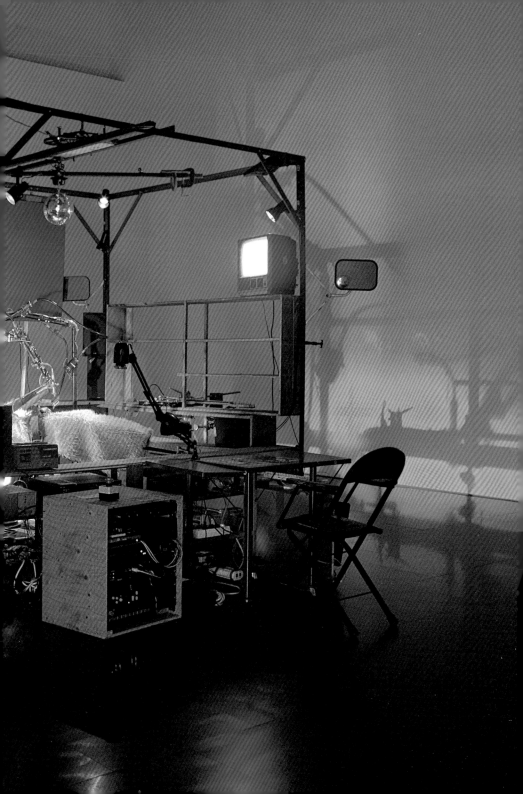

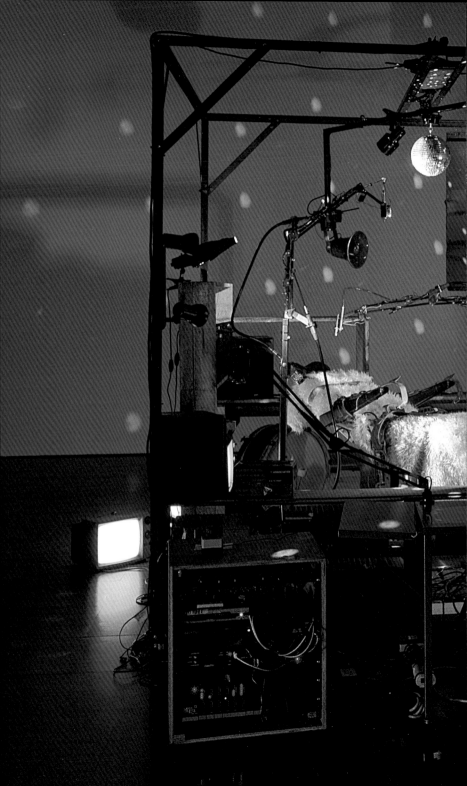

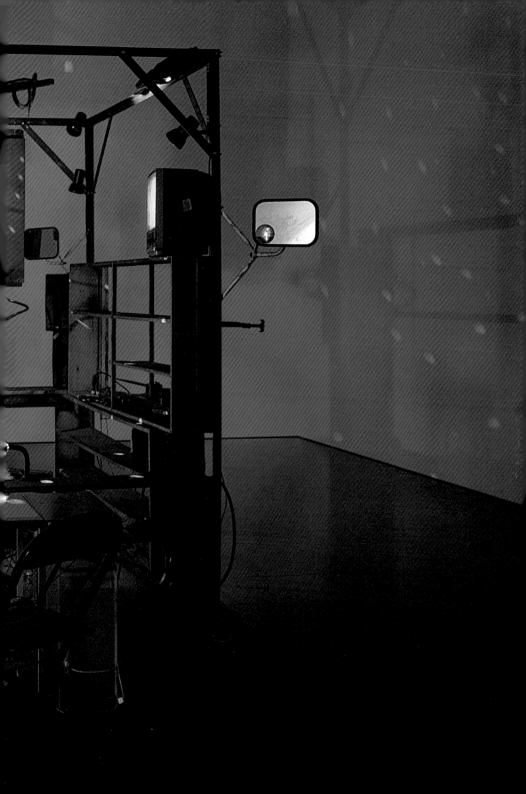

Opera for a Small Room
2005

Mixed media/audio installation
8 record players, 24 speakers, 2,000 records

20 minutes

Road Trip
2004

Mixed media/audio installation
computer-controlled slide projector

15 minutes

Night Canoeing
2004

Video/audio installation

17 minutes

The Muriel Lake Incident
1999

Video projection and binaural audio multimedia construction

5 minutes

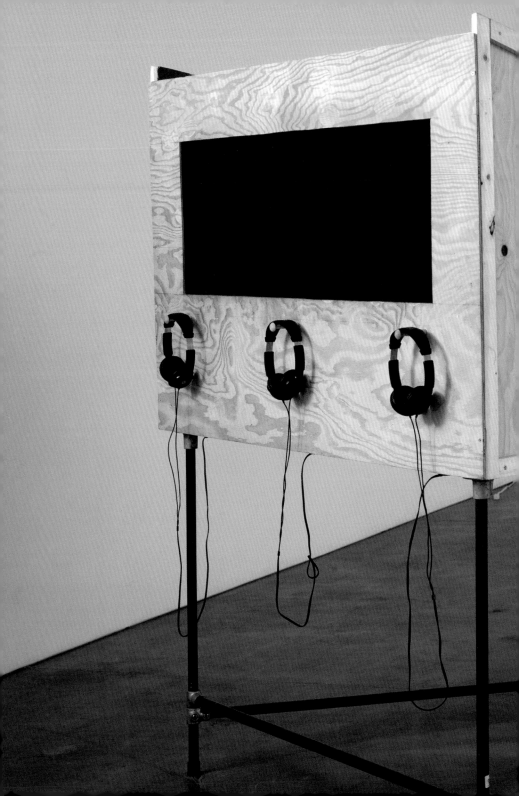

The Dark Pool
1995

Mixed media/audio installation

13 minutes

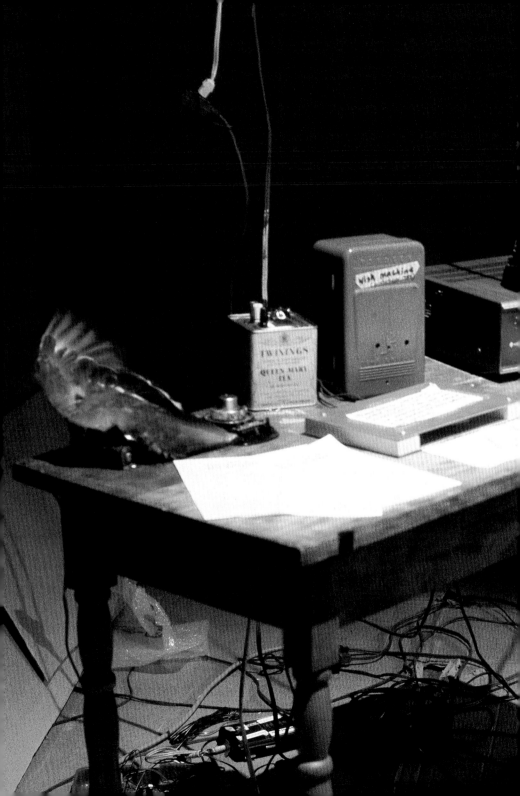

The First House on Maple Street

JULES YOUNGBERG

One day after school, my best friend Jack and I met at our usual meeting place in our clubhouse at the end of Deadpine and where Maple Street begins. No one ever goes to or comes from Maple. Once you get on that road, you're in a different world. It's gloomy and dark, even on a sunny day. We were just sitting in there talking about all the scary stories we've heard about that street. We think the only reason all the other kids on the street try to scare us with those stories is so we will get scared away from our "Maple House" (as we call it) so they can take it over. Then Jack got a grin on his face and that could only mean one thing – he had got another crazy idea.

So I asked him, "What crazy idea have you come up with this time?"

"Nothing," he answered.

"Oh no, there's something alright. I can tell what that face means any day," I stuck to his trail.

He kept trying to keep his case a secret and said, "What face, there's no face… You probably wouldn't want to hear it anyway."

"Tell me."

"Oh alright then, but you could regret this. The only thing is that I dare you to walk up and bang on the door of the first house on Maple Street."

I replied, "That's crazy, that's suicide."

"Not really, because no one has ever been on the other side of the 'Road Line'," he explained.

"That's my point," I told him again.

He explained more and asked, "You're not too scared are you? It's just a little walking and a little banging."

"Of course I'm not. Besides, you're probably right; there's nothing to be afraid of anyway," I started to give in.

"So are you doing it?" he asked one final time.

"Yes. Whatever, I'll do it," I said as I finally gave in.

Once I stepped onto Maple Street I felt sad. It was a sort of vibe the street gave off. I turned to the left and there it was, standing right in front of me: the first house on Maple Street. The old black metal fence was crooked and bent and there were even some holes. There was no gate; it looked like it was torn off. And of course, there it was, lying on the grass all crooked and bent like the fence. The grass was dying and in spots there were flowers, but those were either dead or dying. The cement path up to the house was cracked all over and grass was growing through. The paint was chipped and some shingles from the roof had fallen off and broken. Patches of the grass were covered with shingles. As I walked up the path I thought if Jack was right, maybe I would regret this. Once I got to the top of the stairs I heard Jack yell at me from the gate.

"Come on John. Let's see you do it – you're already there!"

And so there, I did it. I banged on the door of the first house on Maple Street. The door swung open and pushed me to the bottom of the stairs. I heard opera music coming from inside the house. So I walked up the stairs and there was a huge opera going on. It was so much bigger than the house itself. "Hey Jack! You gotta see this!" I yelled.

He ran up and saw it too.

We both said, "Wow," at the same time.

Just then the lady who was singing held a note. It was so loud and for some reason we got sucked in. We just kept moving towards the woman. And finally we went down her throat. Then I landed on a seat in the crowd and Jack landed on the stage. My seat started to grow fur. It became all furry and the crowd faded away. Straps grew and strapped me to the chair. There were two skinny pipes on either side of me and at the top there were other skinny pipes that were attached to them so they could move around. It looked like lights at the end with needles attached to them. They were moving around me and then they started to come towards me.

But as they came towards me it seemed like they weren't because as they came I went down and away. And suddenly I didn't feel the chair any more and I just fell. I fell into darkness and now I was falling through darkness. It seemed like it would never stop and I would just keep on falling for ever. But I was wrong and soon enough I landed on a black floor. At least I think it was black – there was no light so it didn't even look like there was floor. I saw someone in the distance. It looked like Jack. He walked towards me and then started singing. Singing like there were many people singing with him. And slowly he turned into a speaker; a tall black speaker. I turned around and there was another. I turned to each side and they had me surrounded. They made more and more circles until there were forty speakers surrounding me, all singing.

I pushed my way through them and once I got out I couldn't hear them any more. It seemed like they just disappeared. Then a light turned on a little farther up. And that thing that I was in after the opera was there. It looked like there was someone in it. Who? And why are they here? How did they get here? It looked like a kid. I started to run up to it and when I got there I saw Jack sitting there not moving at all. And then he started actually moving, he was trying to get out but then the straps grew and pulled him down. Then the needles started to torture him.

I closed my eyes and screamed, "No!"

In my mind I asked why did I listen to Jack and now why is this house taunting me with him. I opened my eyes and there was a television hanging right in front of me. It looked like there was a tiny person in there. There was. And then he started running towards me. As he ran I noticed that the person was Jack. When he got close enough he just started jumping and the television started swinging. He kept jumping and then finally the television swung at me so hard that it knocked me down.

But when I was supposed to land on my back I just fell right back into that darkness again. I landed in a canoe. There was a person with no face paddling and we were just slowly going down a river in the dark.

I started to hear music, and then before I knew it the river had faded away and at my two sides were two giant speakers playing music. Then the music held one note for a long time. It was high and it reminded me of the opera singer when she did that. It didn't sound very good and when it was going straight to my ears it didn't feel very good either. So I put my hands over my ears and squinted my eyes shut and screamed. All of a sudden I didn't feel the chair any more and just started to fall again. I landed on my stomach and in front of me a little ways further there was a box.

I got up and walked towards it. It was very small and it sounded like there was a record playing so I knelt down and looked inside. It was like an office, there was a chair and then there was the music. A miniature record player was playing and there was the chair and then all sorts of junk all around. I came in to look closer and closer and all of a sudden I was moving so fast and I felt like I was going through some kind of vortex until finally I found myself sitting in the chair inside the box.

On the record there was a picture of a door. The door was surrounded by darkness and there was light coming through. As I stared at it, going in circles, I thought. I thought about what had happened, what was going to happen and then I thought about what could be on the other side of that door. And that was my ticket. The picture started to suck me in.

And I said, "Oh no, not more of this! The sucking, the falling and just this house, please stop."

I found myself standing in the darkness with the door a little ahead of me. I ran up and opened it. All I saw was light. It was so bright that I could barely see. And it was getting brighter and brighter like the sun was getting closer and closer. I knelt down and covered my eyes. Then when I opened them the sun was gone, and Jack was standing beside me and we were standing at the gate of the first house on Maple Street.

Then Jack said, "What are you doing down there? You gonna do it?"

"Do what?" I asked.

"Knock on the door of course! Duh," He answered.

I paused for minute but then I said, "No."

"Really?" he asked.

"Really," I answered.

The End

꙼

Acknowledgements

꙼

Published on the occasion of the exhibition:
Janet Cardiff & George Bures Miller *The House Of Books Has No Windows*

Curated by Fiona Bradley at The Fruitmarket Gallery and by
Andrew Nairne and Suzanne Cotter at Modern Art Oxford.
Assisted by Matt Kelly, Gallery Manager at The Fruitmarket Gallery and
Emily Smith, Exhibition Organiser, Tom Procter-Legg, Gallery Manager
and with additional assistance by Erica Burton, Exhibition Organiser at
Modern Art Oxford

The Fruitmarket Gallery, Edinburgh, 31 July – 28 September 2008
Modern Art Oxford, 14 October 2008 – 18 January 2009

Works courtesy the artists, Galerie Barbara Weiss, Berlin; Luhring Augustine Gallery, New York

Supported by   The Henry Moore Foundation, Outset Contemporary Art Fund,
International Cultural Relations Division at Foreign Affairs and
International Trade Canada (DFAIT) and The Canada House Arts Trust

Published by   The Fruitmarket Gallery
45 Market Street, Edinburgh, EH1 1DF
Tel: +44 (0)131 225 2383 www.fruitmarket.co.uk

Modern Art Oxford
30 Pembroke Street, Oxford, OX1 1BP
Tel + 44 (0)1865 722733 www.modernartoxford.org.uk

Edited by   Fiona Bradley
Designed by   Elizabeth McLean

Photography by Anton Bures, Cardiff & Miller, Markus Tretter, Seber Ugarte & Lorena
Lopez, Jens Ziehe

Distributed by Art Data, 12 Bell Industrial Estate, 50 Cunnington Street, London, W4 5HB
Tel: +44 (0)20 8747 1061 www.artdata.co.uk

ISBN 978–0–9479–1254–3
Printed in the UK by The Creative Group, London

The Henry Moore
Foundation

outset.

Foreign Affairs and
International Trade Canada

THE BANFF CENTRE

The
Fruitmarket
Gallery

Scottish
Arts Council

MODERN ART OXFORD

This book is like a diary of sorts for us, a record of our lives and our working process, and of how our individual sensibilities find their own way into our collaborative work.

JANET CARDIFF, GEORGE BURES MILLER, 2008

Janet Cardiff & George Bures Miller

The House Of Books Has No Windows

VOLUME II
unrealised works

PUBLISHED BY
THE FRUITMARKET GALLERY, EDINBURGH
MODERN ART OXFORD

film or slides projector video

piano sound piece

(f) noise music , people talking , crying
- activities - stereo sound
- different thing on the stage so that
combinations. - one sound after another
= tapes in continual play mode - switch
Just connects electricity

1991

1992

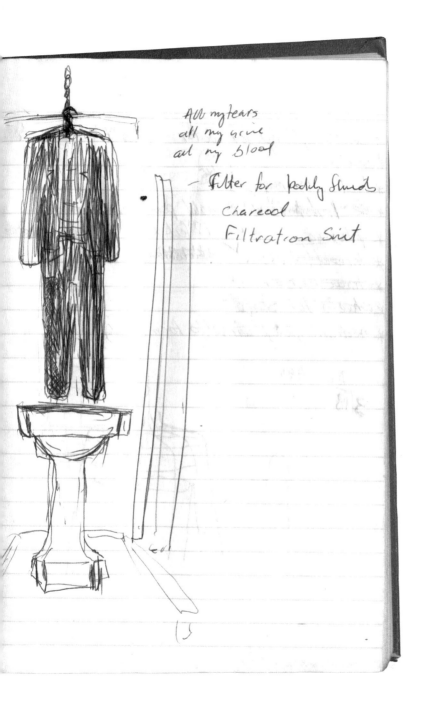

All my tears
all my urine
all my blood

— Filter for bodily fluids
  Charcoal
  Filtration Suit

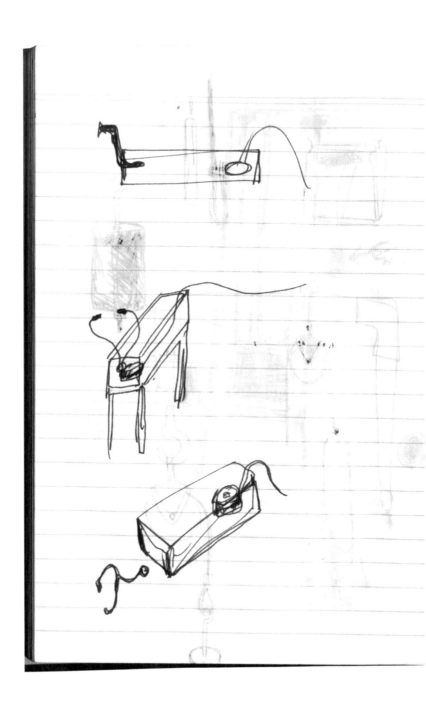

1994

I'm sorry but this was the only way
I could tell you.
Maybe it's stupid but oh well
I don't care
It had to be secret
and untappable
if we were trapped

1994

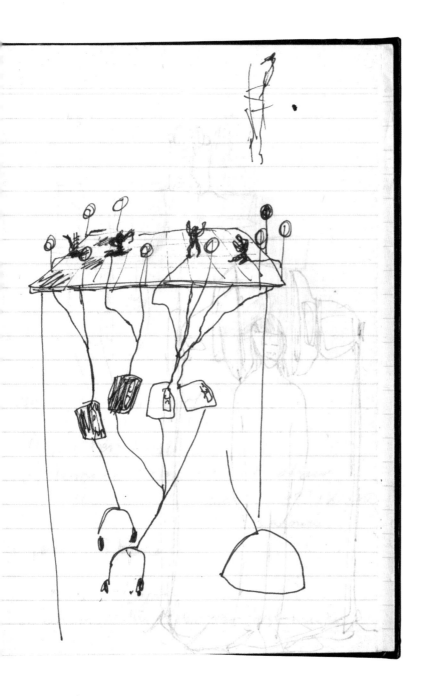

1994

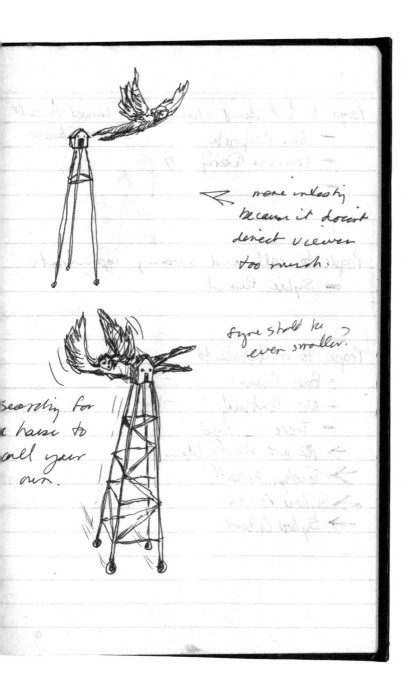

more intesting
because it doesn't
direct viewer
too much.

figure should be
even smaller.

searching for
a house to
call your
own.

etching on old yellowed paper

SIG NAMES

when you turn a page
there is a sound of books dropping or tearing page
or of wings flying
— portraits of people?
~~the~~ sound — me telling stories of each
~~of~~ & of their relationships. or is it
enough to have writing at the bottom.
— weave the characters into a story
— making a narration complex while still making it effective
ineffective

metal ears

metal ears

mouth on spring or not
there at all

— 3D image — 2 people hugging in the
middle of a church or town square

1994

Ideas for Reservoir

~~Reservoir~~

on opposite ends of table

speakers in phones

person playing piano with singing pathetically

do you do you love me anymore do you do you
love me like you did before

~ guitar lick of wild thing
dw ...

gets higher +

1994

1994

Horror Movie

camera for each monitor
Shoots all of the viewers body so
the whole wall moves with the
viewer

1994

plexi
stands

So I decided to be a female cop. I already was female & I liked to follow people so I got all the cop videos that were in the library out and decided that I would have to cut my hair like them, so ~~that was~~ so that was the end of that.

When I had two lovers at the same time I thought of one when I was doing it with the other & vice versa. The grass is always greener on the other side they say but try and find some grass that you can eat without getting hemlock poisoning (simply) — when I was a little girl I had pimples on my teeth. I tried some clarasil but I got a stomach ache ℰ

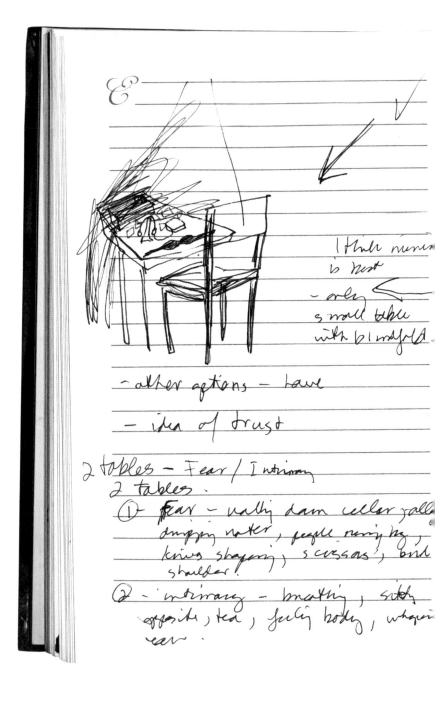

E

I think mirror
is best
– only
small table
with blindfold

– other options – have

– idea of trust

2 tables – Fear / Intimacy
2 tables:
① fear – wally dam cellar, fall
dripping water, people running by,
knives sharpening, scissors, on
shoulder.
② – intimacy – breathing, sitting
opposite, tied, feeling body, whisper
ear.

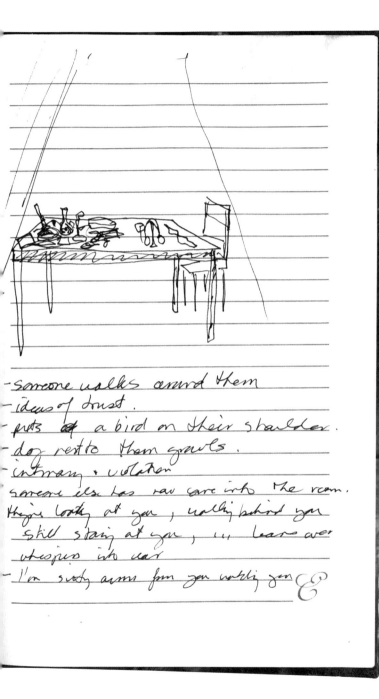

1995

- someone walks around them
- ideas of trust.
- puts a bird on their shoulder.
- dog next to them growls.
- intimacy + violation
someone else has ran came into the room.
they're looking at you, walking behind you
still staring at you, ... leans over
whispers into ear
- I'm sixty arms from you watching you

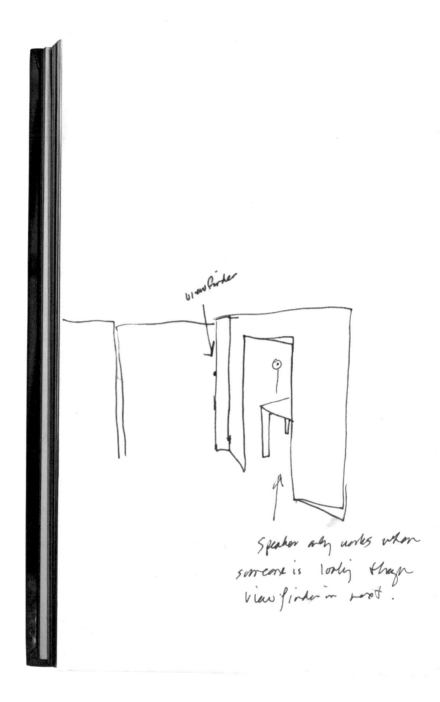

viewfinder

Speaker only works when
someone is looking through
viewfinder in room.

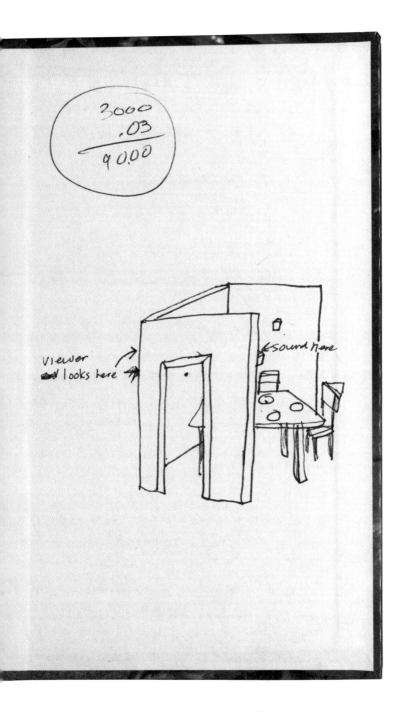

from different speakers
words "But, why?... but, why,"

"I can't tell you that."
tell me again,

- it's about a murder
that happened one night,
~~Ref~~
- the light came in through
the window at the exact
moment ~~that it happened~~
~~or~~ that she spilt her tea on
- you want me to tell you why,
know that; your curious,
OK I'll tell you. It's not a simple
- how's how it happened.
- crazy accordion music of
trapeze music

Judy Garland - somewhere over the
somewhere over the ...
- walking back + forth

g and of Someone
running &
breathing hard.

(Trapeze
music)

1996

did you have a nice day today.
I walked by the river and saw white
swans. Have you ever seen them
fly. My father came into
the house once and told me to
come outdoors with him — He pointed
in the sky and there was a line
of silver. The white of the
swans flying in a V shimmering in
the sun.
I bought some bread today that
had walnuts in it. It tasted
really good. I made a cup of tea
and sat by the window while I
ate my bread.
(then I think we could get onions etc.)
"I told you make sure to check the

nick #14 for Murder

1996

age before you left! Why don't you
even think about what's going to happen.

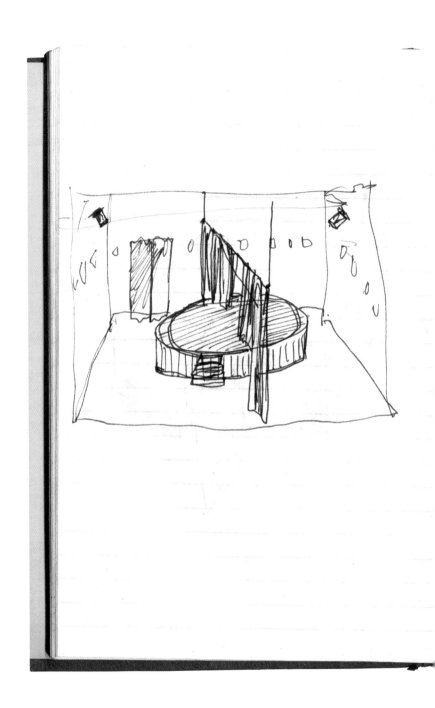

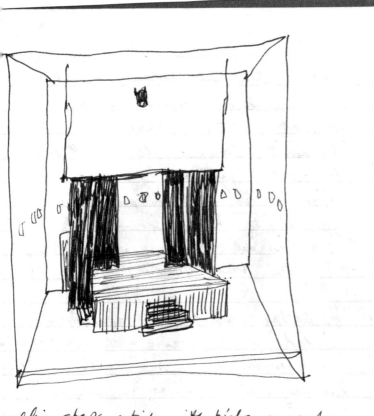

1996

...alking steps outside with birds panned
from left to right in time with size of space
applause from several speakers
Shakespearean theatre @ stars tally to
person who triggers — perhaps thousand
through 3-D Q sound?
Spotlights come on in persons face
- maybe at same time as applause?

1996

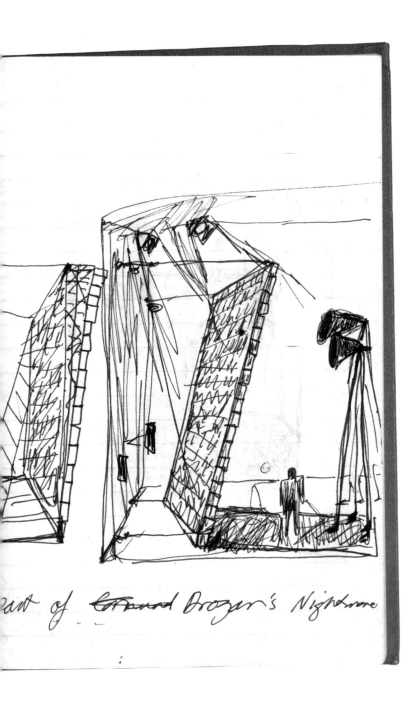

Part of Edward Drozen's Nightmare

1996

Bed of Books

creaking noise
once in a while
like this is fading

16

16'

spotlight

voice is
projected to
here

talking noise below - 8 track 8 speakers

...glish voice then german translation
"...tle says that when she was young she
...od right doorways

The House of Books Has No Windows

about the picture such as - "so
that are you going to do, just sit
here and look out the window" - was
I said so that it involves them
that only it becomes a new
kind of sculptural space or
dealing with a mental
3-D space - putting your
mind into the environment
sculpture does that really
well - relate to the
imaginary space. Because
in memory we 3-D we
are to use our memory
to know what is on the
the side of a sculpture.
- it is not the message it
is the medium - the hardest
pieces

1996

- picture of ... that farm ... ?
- scientific needs of attempts at genetic farming of humans with animals.

- Muybridge-like studies of Helen running with drawing overlay of a human form (with mask)
- small video of merging of bark and growl

- stories of personal interaction carrying out of speakers in table.

- running somato things careless. paintings and breaths of dog
- video of running from viewpoint of dog

- about questions of representation & what it is to be human

1996

1996

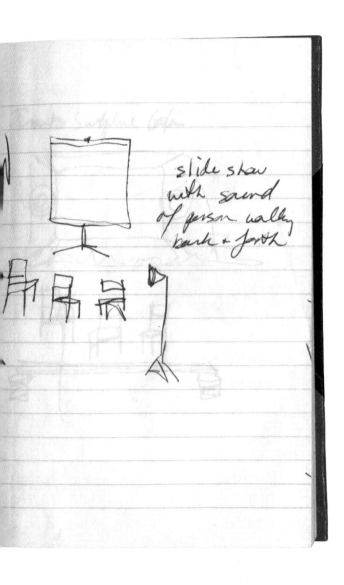

slide show
with sound
of person walking
back + forth

1996

1996

1996

an said that you were going
the store for milk

1996

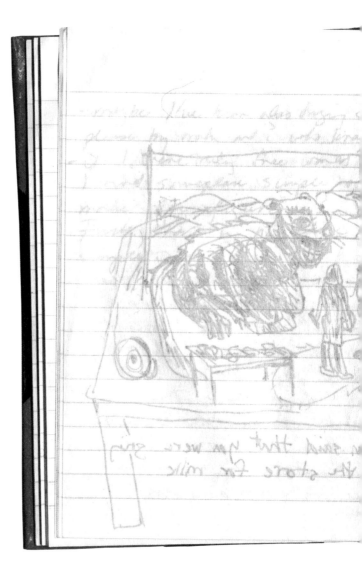

I saw a cloud today
that looked like a
penis

1996

Have you seen my sock?

Stereo Video
Ideas

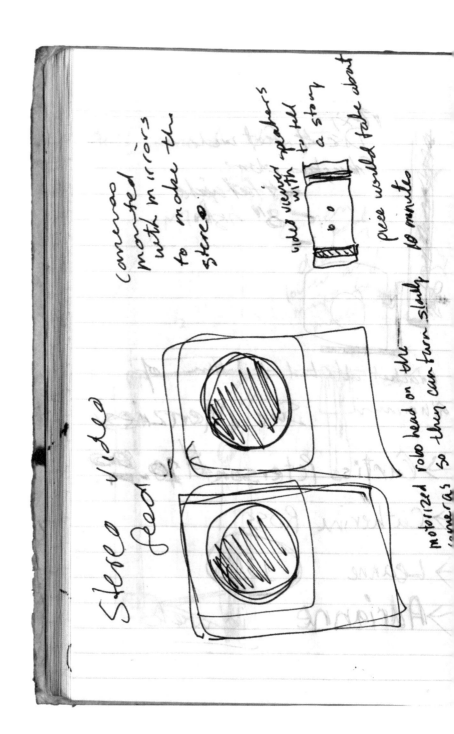

cameras
mounted
with mirrors
to make the
stereo

video viewed with speakers
to tell
a story

piece would take about
10 minute

motorized robo head on the
cameras so they can turn slowly

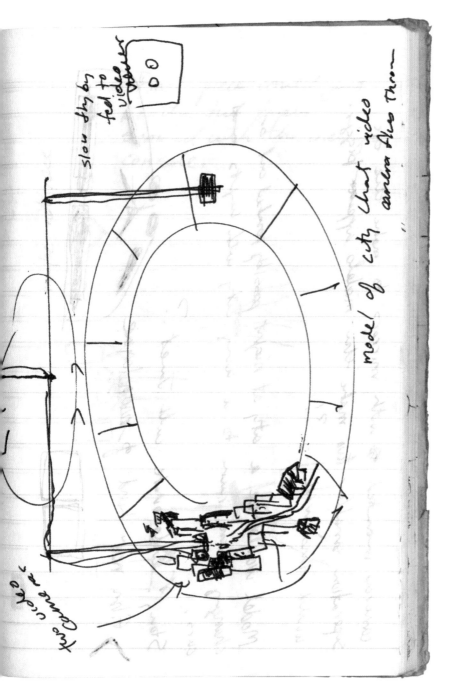

slow thy by feel to video viewer

model of city that video camera flies thru

two cameras

1996

1997

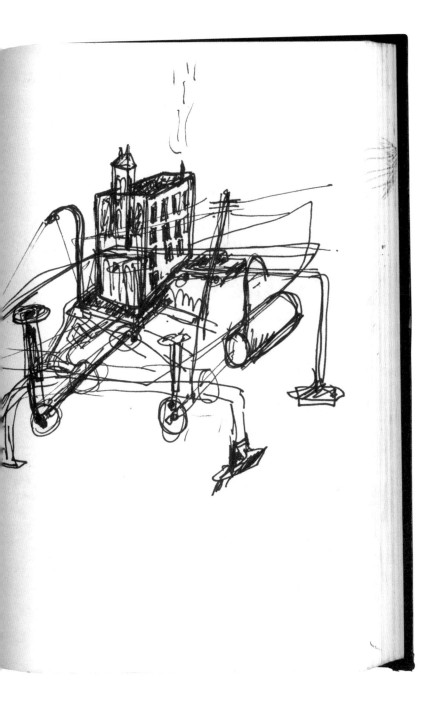

sand of walking getting ready to leave
going door, closing

1997

1997

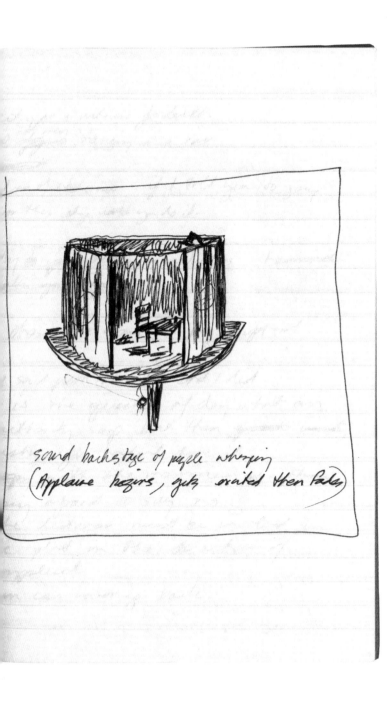

sound backstage of people whispering
(Applause begins, gets excited then fades)

One night when I was asleep the
rat put it's nose by my ear
and sniffed and then ran across
my back when I screamed.

You said ~~you were scared of me~~!
scared you away! I ~~smothered~~ you...
miss you.
walk around the table ~~and rubber gloves on~~
~~get put out of cage~~ ~~be~~ ~~they~~ ~~again~~

Since that night I haven't slept
very well. I keep ~~sorry~~ hearing thing
(going cage)
So I bought myself a rat to get
rid of my fear. It's a female
named Sarah.
    (get out rat)
I do drawing of her so I can learn to love
(put Mahalia Jackson record on)
I still can't touch her with my bare hand
    (go towards scared person)
~~Today didn't~~ How can you just stop
        loving me? It's not fair

1997

1997

"Sitting in an Empty Room"

there may be from ceiling

1997

- mystery figure walks up behind and talks to the person
- need to have them sit down only one at a time

angles

I in an empty room.

walls in and around the person a bit.
There was an empty house ~~then~~ on
one of my fathers farms that I used
to play in "

~~Everseroooos ~~ there wasn't any furniture
wet wooden floors and plaster walls, "dark rooms.
                        and light rooms.
Birds would get trapped in these rooms
" sort of birds " flying from darkness to light.

There were ghost images on the windows from
~~there~~ their attempts to get out - where
they had thrown their bodies against
the glass
~~broken glass ?~~)

~~Pernit~~
Do you remember when we ~~and~~
went there one day and you asked to

1997

3 Sunday

123–242

"Le Cirque d'amour fou"
"The Circus of (attempts at love)"
— great feats of courage.
— leaps of faith.

**Rudyard Kipling,
Indian-born British
writer (1865-1936)**
Writing to a magazine that
had published his obituary:
I've just read that I am dead.
Don't forget to delete me
from your list of subscribers.
Anekdotenschatz
(Hoffmeister)

— projections inside tent · theatre of illusion
— tent of memories.

— tunnel of fear
— scaffolding of unknowing

— contrast between the sounds of a real
circus + crowds + the empty spa

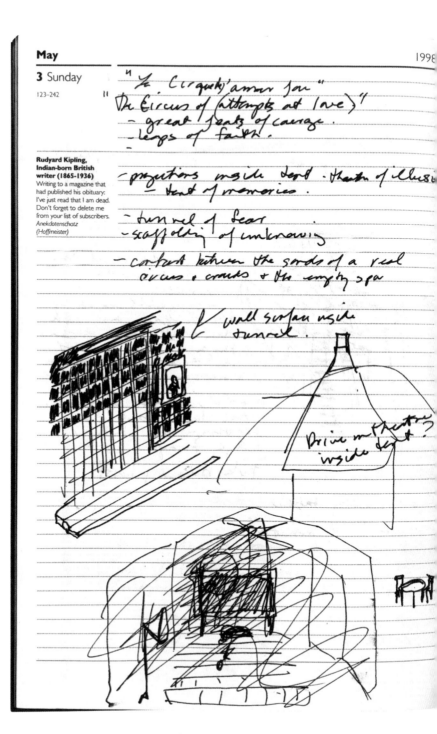

wall surface inside
tunnel.

Prime mover theatre
inside tent?

Musée

May

Wk	M	T	W	T	F	S	S
18					1	2	3
19	4	5	6	7	8	9	10
20	11	12	13	14	15	16	17
21	18	19	20	21	22	23	24
22	25	26	27	28	29	30	31

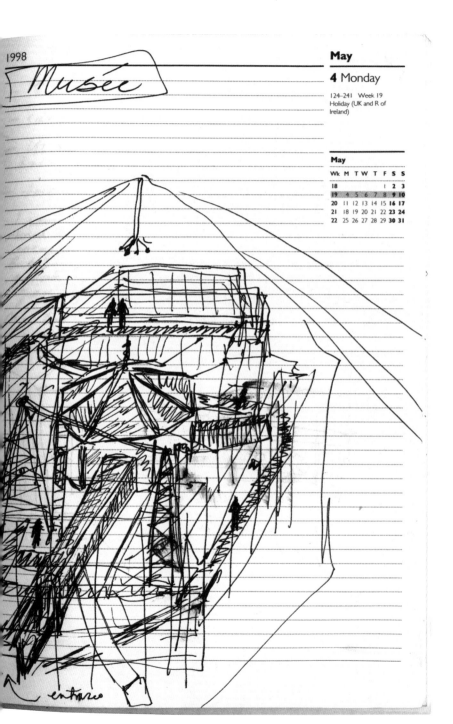

1998

entrée

1998

Theatre Piece

June 9 / 98

Just thought of an idea I thought would be brilliant

May

Wk	M	T	W	T	F	S	S
18					1	2	3
19	4	5	6	7	8	9	10
20	11	12	13	14	15	16	17
21	18	19	20	21	22	23	24
22	25	26	27	28	29	30	31

– all the lights go off – people wear headsets play with people whispering.
– voice starts to tell story.
– take them elsewhere through the sound.
– then the lights pop on + someone on stage is intensely singing (lights are focused on the singer) then lights cut out again.
– then like floptrone there could be a singer on stage that interacts with the audio in the headset.

– performers come on + off – they are all wacky + bad.
– # like a variety theatre
    – cowboy poet.
    – insane dead woman dog having a sing

– change the way the audience behaves – the audience chants + boos or throws things
    – person sells them to throw things
"marshmallow theatre"

– some performers talk to audience – everything is
            cued to the soundtrack
this could be live but it could also be a 30 minute laser disc piece.

1998

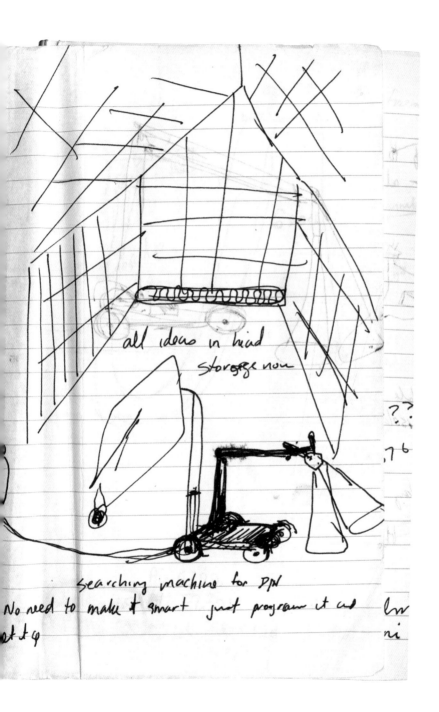

all ideas in head
storage now

searching machine for DPN

No need to make it smart just program it and
let it go

1998

Alludes to but not
as, this is too many

greenhouse —
oxygen Tent —

51" high
20⁴ wide

1998

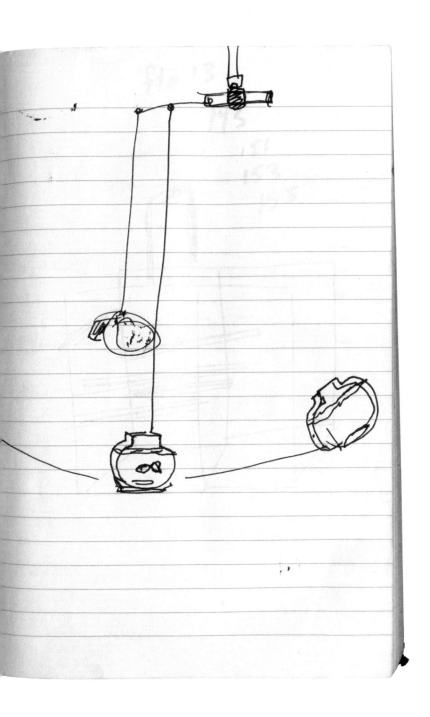

1998

Night flight

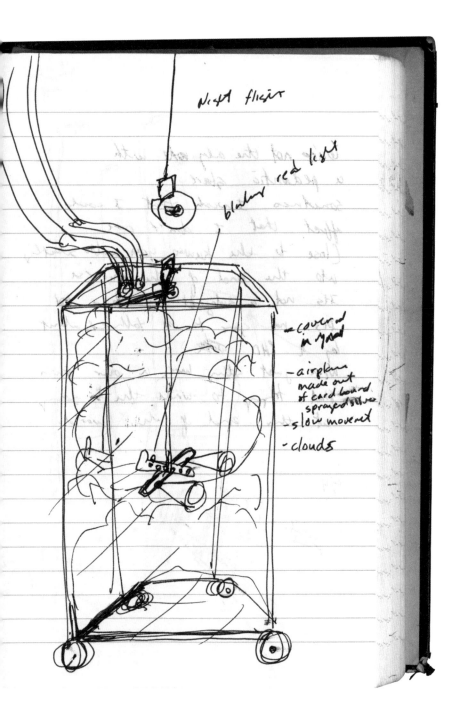

blinking red light

- covered
  in gray

- airplane
  made out
  of card board
  sprayed silver
- slow movement

- clouds

– 79 –

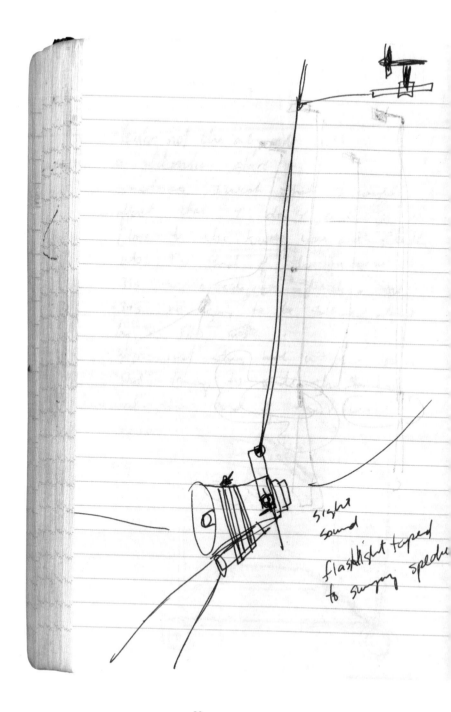

sight
sound
flashlight taped
to swinging speaker

1998

1998

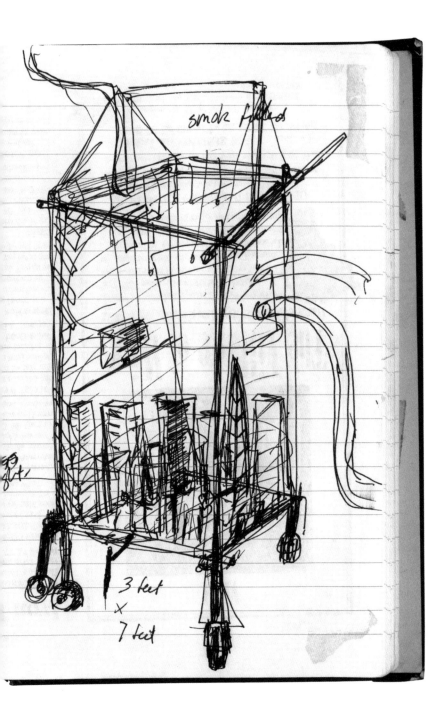

smoke filled

3 feet
x
7 feet

1998

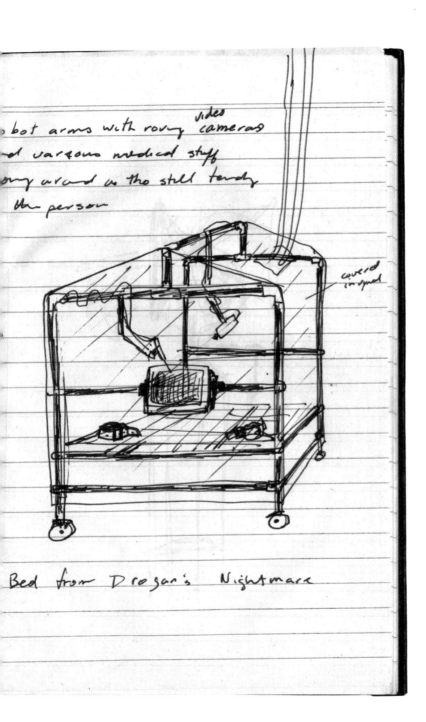

...bot arms with roving video cameras
...d various medical stuff

...ony around as tho still tends
the person

covered
in vynyl

Bed from Drogan's Nightmare

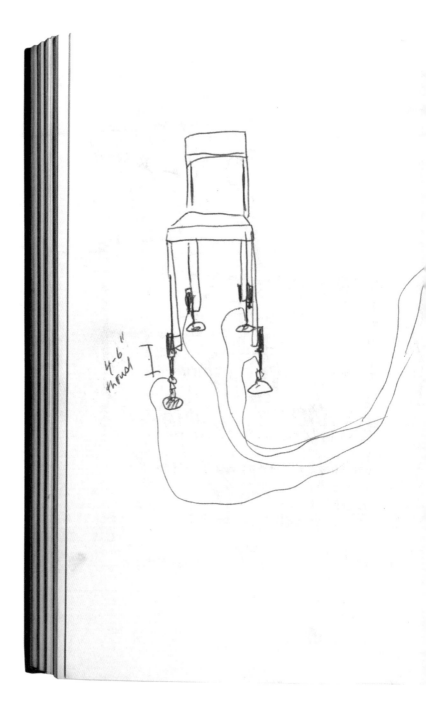

4-6"
thrust

RAINmaker

1999

→ Prototype for room piece
at least 20 chairs all
spreed up

1999

spotlight

chair gets let
down slowly into
black ink — there
is a hole in the floor
beneath
— orchestral music.
dramatic/scary or

— chair disappears into ink
— person gasping sound
— or maybe silence

1999

1999

Hollow nose urethan
later cover &
cloth

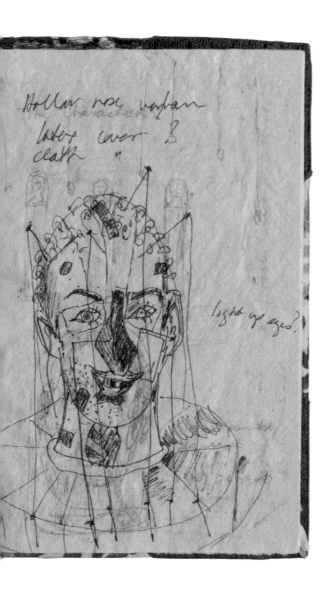

light up eyes?

1999

eaty a world of characters.
strange simulacrums of
people

glass
eyes

T.V. lips

me Sally about sexual desire

1999

1999

simple shadow
piece

RIDE to what the ??
Move to ~~ee~~ find a building that
could be converted. Pimps low water

2000

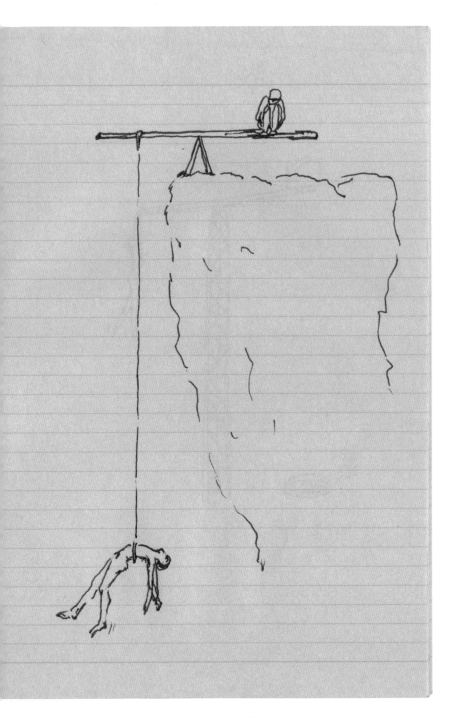

2000

2000

2000

2001

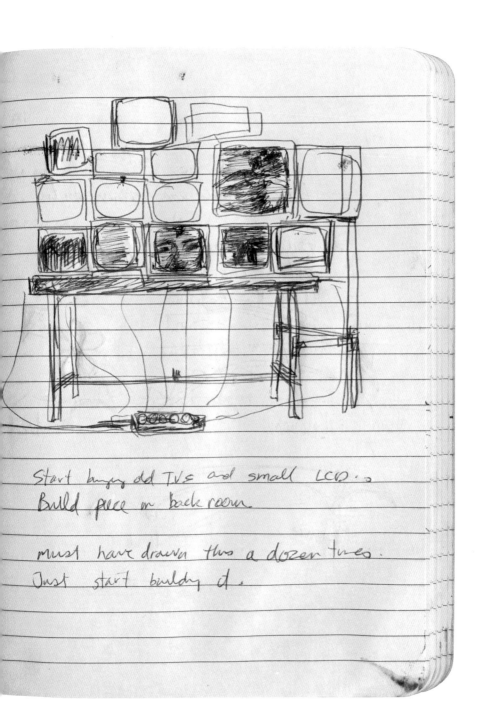

Start buying old TVs and small LCDs.
Build piece in back room.

must have drawn this a dozen times.
Just start building it.

2002

— moral dilema? its not hitchcock.

4 part structure
   B   A - Isabelle & sounds - claustrophobia
       B - opera singer — in theatre? or studio?
       C - man making model house — small cluttered space
       D - walking in snow theme — great expanse
                — person calling behind
   — find out structure of opera.

A B A B C A B C D A B C D A

A - Isabelle kitchen — boiling eggs ✓
                      — sounds build
B - singer putting on record + empty room ✓
A - Isabelle listening to wall ✓
B - singer walking around room singing along.
C - man building a house — zoom into
        small rooms — puts small woman into room
                     — sand walks around ✓
B/A - shot of Isabelle standing in same place
  ✓ walks and puts egg on table — table starts to shake
  ✓ — Isabelle turns moves away to watch it.
C — man shaking house then blows on it ✓
A — Isabelle throws pillow — starts huffy
  ✓   pillow — fighting it around the space
  ✓ — drumming sand builds up —
✓ D — pillow bursts, feathers. come down slowly
✓ C — man pours sugar over house
✓ D — door goes to snow scene
   B — sand of singer

2002

Luigi Nono

Opera ...

A – Isabelle in apartment doing very simple acts, washing
    hands – boiling eggs – buttering toast
    – hears noise ~~close~~ looks scared moves around room

✹ – noise builds – screen goes black.

B – walking feet sound – fade up to singer eating toast
    camera turns around sees singer – singer walks to
    put on record – close up of record of Moratti

A – Isabelle listening to wall with glass in bed
    (lying face down in bed with ear to glass) turns over again

B – puts record on again song starts again, sings with
    it – walks around space
    – darkness – sound of singer walking around

C – light goes on quickly – man in small room
    sits down to table – builds model house
    – takes tweezers + small female figure – puts her
    into house – camera slowly zooms in + moves
    around looking through windows of model

A – Isabelle standing in space

  – the singing should not be just opera – it should be
    a wild voice moving into drums + other
    voices – use Isobel's voice as well?

  – puts on big fur coat + muffler + boots in apartment
    at end. → as if she's going for walk.
  – walks back + forth in room around in big circle.
  – she talks to the wall about ~~being in a restaurant~~ thirty
    ~~and~~ about someplace and your body feels it

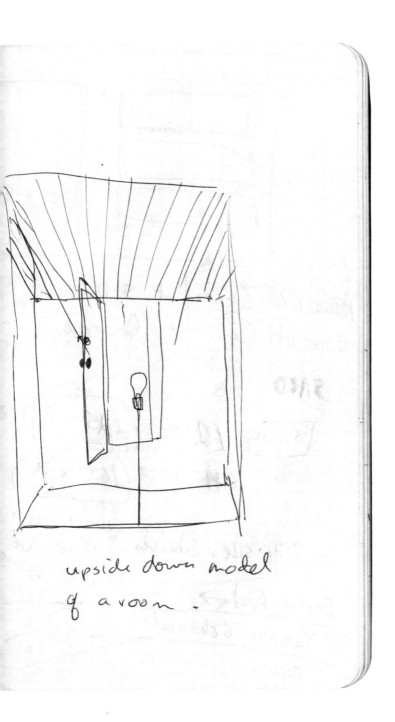

upside down model
of a room.

2003

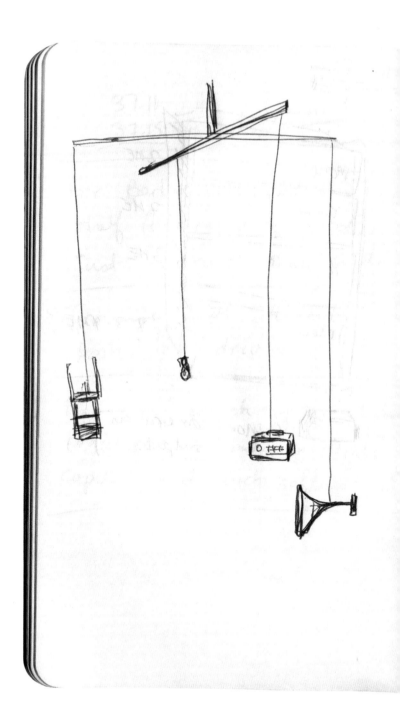

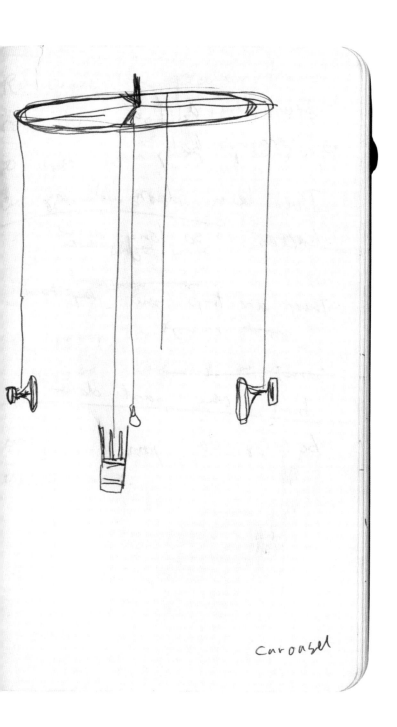

carousel

2003

rum solo
udi controlled drum kit
se

trait - Ringo ?
- research motion control
    - stepper motors most easy
        to program for velocity
        & motion ??

tach at old
apparatus.   (Computer

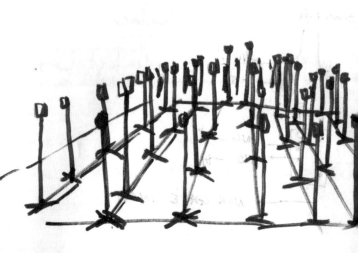

2003

3000 speakers ?!
Vocal compositions sweeps
through the space (like wa

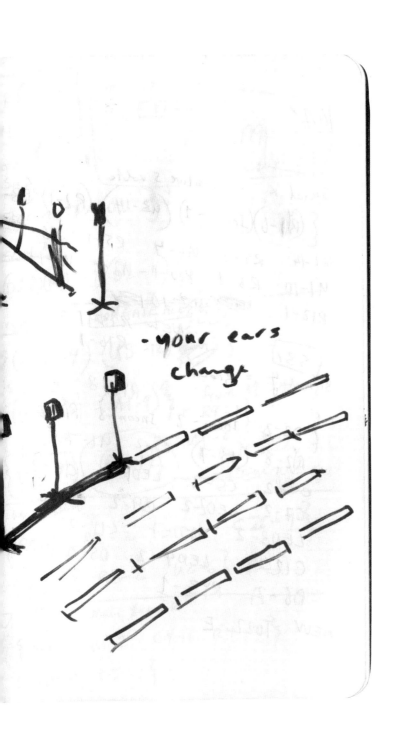

-your ears
change

2004

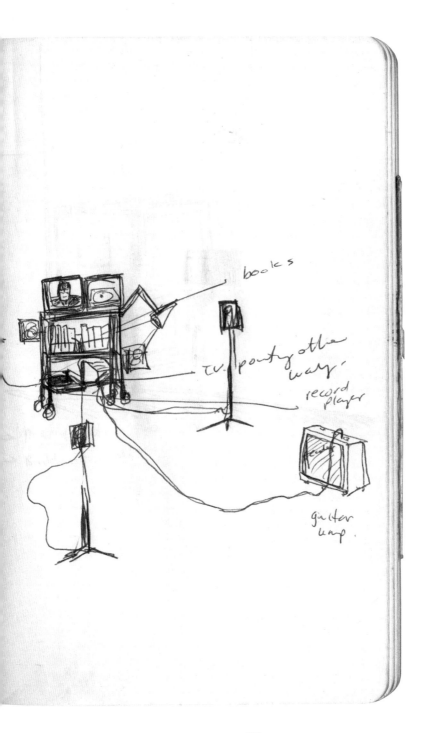

books

tv. pointyy otha
way.

record
player

guitar
amp.

2004

Duet

Domine with suitar fr

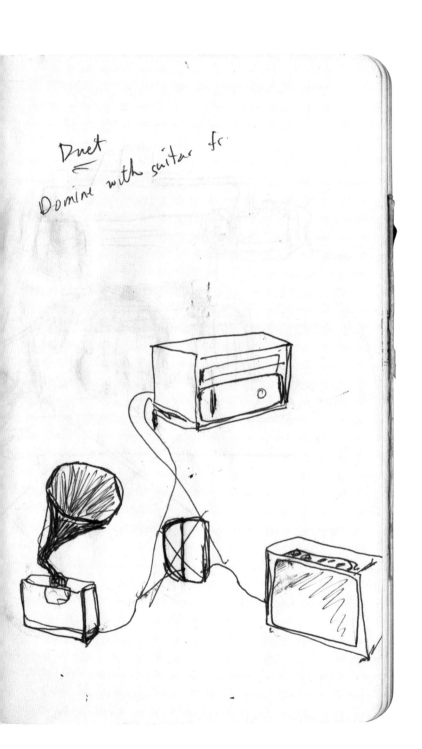

2004

Pick up Truck fountain –

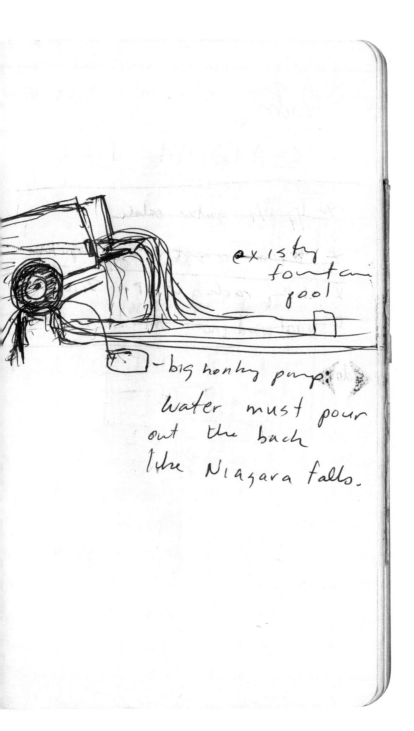

existg
fountain
pool

—big honkg pump

Water must pour
out the back
like Niagara falls.

Speakers in drawer come
on whe drawers opened.

another one could be
sounds of locations recorded

videos telly stores
and music.

2004

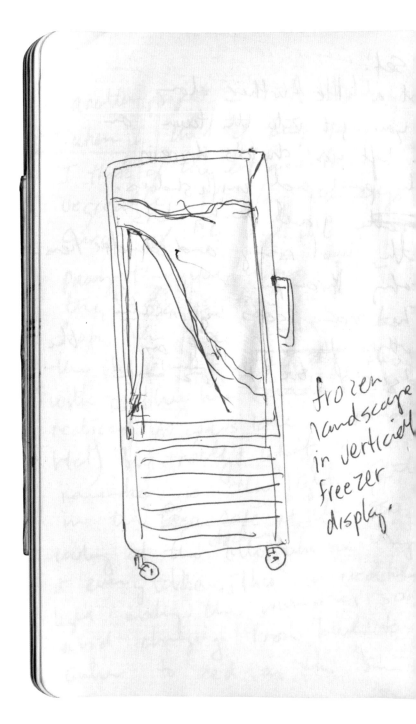

frozen
landscape
in vertical
freezer
display.

To take to London
- DVD
- Data Bank + power supply
- s video cable.
- suit jacket P.S.
-

how would
they age →
freezer burn

Could you ~~freeze a~~ cut
ice out of frozen water
falls and display them.
how and
it effect them.

2006

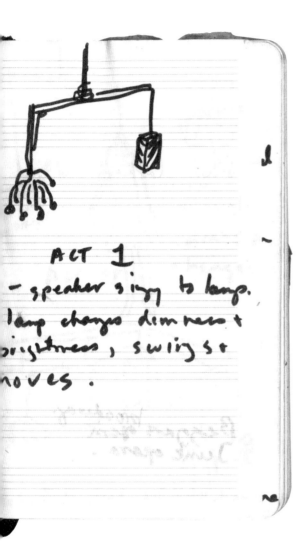

ACT 1
- speaker sings to lamp.
lamp changes dimness &
brightness, swings &
moves.

2006

turning wheel

or just a

dress on

a hanger

ACT II

r doll
Brazil

aby Baby don't get hooked on me

NY

– if Open in big space then small rooms shall be quiet? – architectural works
– secret hotel.

3 window pieces ī sand

3 photographs

1 model for head. – library?

merz / memory palace

or

1 box of babel

1 light chairs + sort of whispers + footsteps.

2006

The Undressing

hidden screened sort — seems like
has walking around.
— small room — life-size figures projected.
all voice — guy directs for
undressing — different people
— woman, man,
what to ask — older woman, young woman

The Dancer.

W + M's voice giving order to
2 dancers M+F. They put on
various music + tell them
to show more pain.
- She dances until exhausted.
They yell faster!
= very S+M in way.

voice say - we're hungry - can't
we come and now
J - no you have to stay.

2006

- street ~~not~~ watch for cars
  both ways

each key is a sample of
a scream or cry

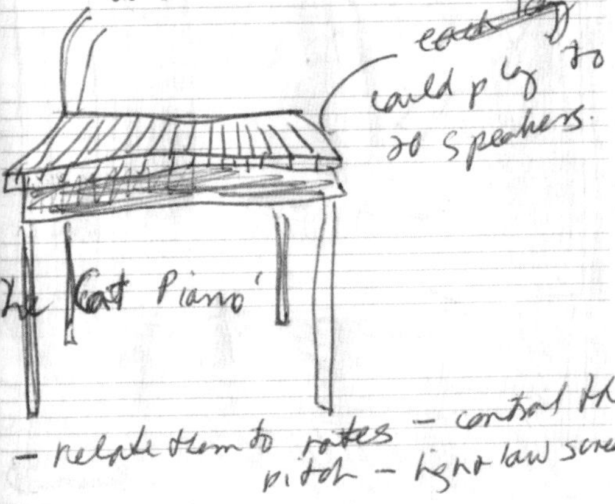

~~each key~~
each key
could play to
20 speakers

The 'cat Piano'

- relate them to notes — control the
  pitch — light law screens.

◦≫≪◦

The End

◦≫≪◦